A DAY IN THE LIFE OF A
Commercial Fisherman

by John F. Klein and Carol Gaskin
Photography by John F. Klein

Troll Associates

Library of Congress Cataloging in Publication Data

Klein, John F. (John Frederick), (date)
  A day in the life of a commercial fisherman.

    Summary: Follows a commercial fisherman through his
day as he prepares his boat for a two-week fishing
trip, leaves port in the Gulf of Mexico, operates
navigational equipment and a sonar "fish finder,"
and unloads the day's catch.
    1. Fishers—Juvenile literature. [1. Fishers.
2. Brown, Mark, Captain.   3. Occupations]
I. Gaskin, Carol.   II. Title.
HD8039.F65K57   1988   639'.2'02373   87-10949
ISBN 0-8167-1109-7 (lib. bdg.)
ISBN 0-8167-1110-0 (pbk.)

The author and publisher wish to thank Mark Brown, captain of the *Kaye-D*,
and Curt Esmond, the mate, for their cooperation and advice.

Mark Brown is a commercial fisherman and captain of his own boat, the *Kaye-D*. He fishes throughout the year in the Gulf of Mexico off the coast of Florida. Mark plans each new fishing trip while returning from the last, because his short time in port is always busy.

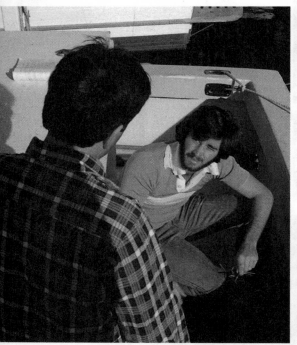

At the marina, Mark and his first mate work together to fix a problem with the *Kaye-D*'s steering. Curt makes an adjustment in the "stern," or rear, of the boat. He is an excellent mechanic as well as an able mate and fisherman. This is important at sea, where there are no repair shops.

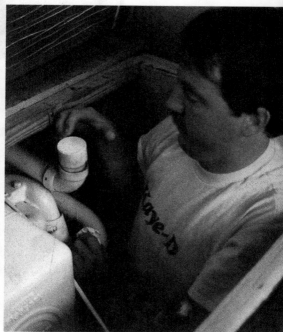

While Curt finishes the repair, Mark checks the tackle and supplies, and he stocks the pantry with enough food for a two-week trip. Once at sea, he and Curt will be on their own, so Mark's preparations are thorough. After a final check of the engine, they are ready to leave port.

Mark pilots the *Kaye-D* to the "fish house," a fish wholesaler and supply business, where he buys 200 gallons of fuel, 700 pounds of ice and 750 pounds of bait. The bait, which is frozen mullet and sardines, will be loaded into a giant cooler, or "fish box," built into the deck of the boat.

Curt protects his ears from the noise of the ice blower while he and Mark pack the fish box with layers of ice and bait. As bait is used and the catch of the day is stored, the six bins of the fish box will be rearranged many times.

"Let's go fishing!" Mark says, steering the *Kaye-D* out to sea. It's a day's ride to the fishing grounds, and Mark uses sophisticated equipment to help him navigate. But as an experienced captain, he also relies on his sharp eyesight, a good compass, and a steady hand at the wheel.

One of Mark's most useful tools is the "loran," or "long-range navigation," system. The numbers on the loran unit tell Mark exactly where he is. Mark also depends on his radar, sonar, and long-range and short-range radios. This equipment helps assure him of a safe trip and a good catch.

While Mark steers, Curt prepares bait for tomorrow's fishing. It takes most of the afternoon to fillet 250 pounds of mullet and to slice the fillets into V-shaped chunks. Working with a knife is dangerous on a rolling boat, so he wraps his fingers in tape to protect them.

Toward evening, Mark consults his sonar "fish finder." From the shadows on the graph paper, he can tell the ocean depth and bottom contour. He notes loran numbers in places he thinks he'll find fish. He also calls other fishermen on the radio to find out where the fish have been biting.

At sunset, Mark shuts off the engine and enjoys the quiet. He studies his log book, a captain's most prized possession. His daily entries in the log record the weather, tides, and locations where fish have been caught. He had good luck in this spot last month—1200 pounds of fish in just two days!

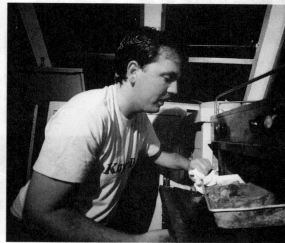

It's dinner time and Mark is the cook. He has learned to prepare a variety of dishes in the *Kaye-D*'s tiny galley. Mark and Curt have time for only one hot meal a day, so it must be a good one. Tonight it will be steak, salad, and baked potatoes.

Before going to bed, Mark does a safety check. He uses radar to locate other boats and ships in the area. He tells the boats nearby that he is "bedding down" for the night. Then he makes up the bunks. The radio will stay on all night, in case of an emergency.

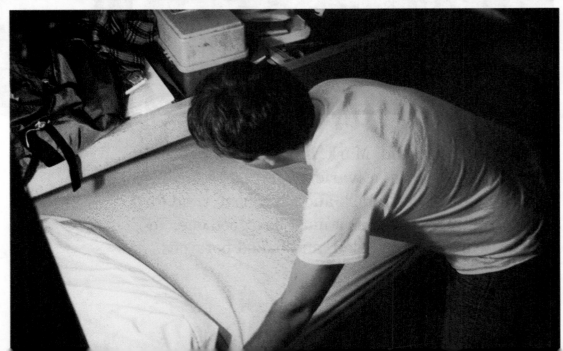

Curt pulls the anchor at dawn. It's time for work!
He wraps his fingers with duct tape before baiting
hundreds of fishhooks. The sea is rough and he
must be careful of the sharp barbs on the hooks.
Chunks of mullet will be used to bait some hooks,
while whole sardines will be used on others.

Mark cuts more bait while Curt adjusts the *Kaye-D*'s reel to let out line smoothly. The giant reel works much like a small sport-fishing reel, but it can hold up to eighteen miles of extra-strong line! That's why this type of fishing is called "long lining."

Mark guides the line off the reel as the *Kaye-D* moves slowly along on autopilot. In the stern, Curt marks the beginning of the line with an orange float. Mark lets out 200 feet of line, enough to reach from the float to the ocean bottom. Then Curt adds metal weights to sink the line.

The *Kaye-D* moves forward, letting out over a mile of line. Curt puts 800 baited hooks on the line in the next forty minutes—one hook every three seconds! Always looking down, he chooses each hook from the bait box and clips it on by feel as the line whizzes by.

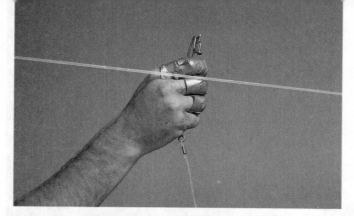

Steel clips attach the baited hooks to the line. Curt squeezes the clip, puts it on the line, and instantly pulls his hand out of the way. He is very careful because if his hand gets caught on a hook, he can be pulled overboard.

As soon as Mark and Curt are finished "setting" the line, they unhook the end of the line from the reel and circle back to the orange float. They fasten the beginning of the line to the reel and pull in their catch. Today they are lucky. The first hook yields a beautiful red snapper. Sometimes they even catch two fish at one time.

Not every fish is a "keeper." Mark measures a red grouper against a yardstick he has fastened to the side of the boat. It is under the legal limit, so he throws it back. Later they catch a barracuda. Its sharp teeth are dangerous, but they save it for bait.

At the end of the first line, Mark feels a huge tug, and up comes a forty-pound Warsaw grouper. It's been a good haul. Mark and Curt work quickly so they can get the line out again before the fish move. But first, the catch must be unhooked and cleaned.

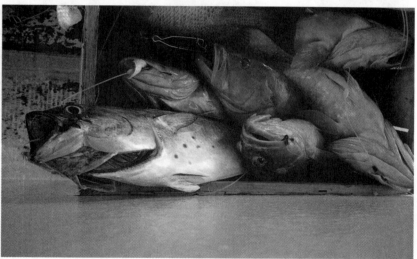

Mark stores the cleaned fish loosely on ice until the end of the day. The next line brings in an average amount of fish, about 125 pounds. This time there are red grouper and two kinds of snapper, all "good eating" fish. Mark has caught over twenty kinds of fish on one trip.

On the way to set the next line, Curt spots a "pod," or small family group, of playful dolphins. These marine mammals love boats, and are a pleasure to watch as they leap into the air and frolic in the *Kaye-D*'s wake. "They are the best fishermen in the Gulf of Mexico!" laughs Mark.

Mark and Curt continue to fish past sunset and into the night. Mark is reluctant to quit as long as the fish are biting, but by ten o'clock they are hungry, tired and dirty. They have had a good day, pulling in lots of red grouper.

While Mark cooks, Curt unloads the day's catch, nearly 600 pounds, from the icy fish box. Then he neatly packs the bigger fish, head to tail, at the bottom of one bin. He layers fish and ice until the catch is tightly packed in the bins. Among fishermen, fish-packing is considered an art.

26

After eight full days of fishing, Mark decides it's time to go home. He has heard on his radio from other fishermen that fish prices are dropping. He wants to get in before the prices drop any further, so he travels through the night to reach the fish house by morning.

Just after dawn, Curt cleans the *Kaye-D*. He scrubs the deck and the outside of the fish box with a strong disinfectant to remove slippery fish scales and seaweed. Then he hangs the empty hooks in the sun to dry. When he is finished, he washes his hands in a bucket of bleach to prevent infection.

Back at the fish house, Mark helps lower a conveyor to the fish box on his boat. The catch is unpacked and sent up the conveyor to a scale. Mark will now find out exactly what his catch weighs, and how much the fish house is paying.

Mark's fish are weighed, separated by type, and put into boxes on ice. Mark checks with the man who works the scales to see that their totals agree. His catch amounts to 2800 pounds—not bad for a short trip. Now he must complete the transaction.

In the business office, the bookkeeper tells Mark that he was wise to come in early. Other fish houses in the area have dropped the price they are paying for fish, and the prices here will be lowered tomorrow. Mark agrees to the offered price and sells his catch here. Now he can pay Curt for his share of the catch.

Mark loves the freedom of being an independent commercial fisherman. He began as a mate and worked hard to buy his own boat. As he watches another golden sunset, he dreams of someday owning a whole fleet of fishing boats. But for now he is satisfied. He feels at home on the *Kaye-D*, with the smell of salt air and the sounds of the sea.